The award-winning pictures gathered in this diary have been drawn from the archives of the Wildlife Photographer of the Year competition – the international showcase for the very best nature photography. The competition is owned by the Natural History Museum, London, which prides itself on revealing and championing the diversity of life on Earth.

Wildlife Photographer of the Year is one of the most popular of the Museum's exhibitions. Visitors come not only to see breathtaking imagery, but also to understand some of the threats faced by our planet's animals and plants. Understanding and finding ways of conserving the Earth's biodiversity are at the heart of the Museum's work. This exhibition is one way to share that mission with others, encouraging us to see the environment around us with new eyes.

The Natural History Museum looks after a world-class collection of over 80 million specimens. It is also a leading scientific research institution, with ground-breaking projects in more than 68 countries. About 350 scientists work at the Museum, researching the valuable collections to better understand life on Earth. Every year more than five million visitors, of all ages and levels of interest, are welcomed through the Museum's doors.

2021

JANUARY

wk	M	T	W	Th	F	S	S
1					1	2	3
2	4	5	6	7	8	9	10
3	11	12	13	14	15	16	17
4	18	19	20	21	22	23	24
5	25	26	27	28	29	30	31

FEBRUARY

wk	M	T	W	Th	F	S	S
6	1	2	3	4	5	6	7
7	8	9	10	11	12	13	14
8	15	16	17	18	19	20	21
9	22	23	24	25	26	27	28

MARCH

wk	M	T	W	Th	F	S	S
10	1	2	3	4	5	6	7
11	8	9	10	11	12	13	14
12	15	16	17	18	19	20	21
13	22	23	24	25	26	27	28
14	29	30	31				

APRIL

wk	M	T	W	Th	F	S	S
14				1	2	3	4
15	5	6	7	8	9	10	11
16	12	13	14	15	16	17	18
17	19	20	21	22	23	24	25
18	26	27	28	29	30		

MAY

wk	M	T	W	Th	F	S	S
18						1	2
19	3	4	5	6	7	8	9
20	10	11	12	13	14	15	16
21	17	18	19	20	21	22	23
22	24	25	26	27	28	29	30
23	31						

JUNE

wk	M	T	W	Th	F	S	S
23		1	2	3	4	5	6
24	7	8	9	10	11	12	13
25	14	15	16	17	18	19	20
26	21	22	23	24	25	26	27
27	28	29	30				

JULY

wk	M	T	W	Th	F	S	S
27				1	2	3	4
28	5	6	7	8	9	10	11
29	12	13	14	15	16	17	18
30	19	20	21	22	23	24	25
31	26	27	28	29	30	31	

AUGUST

wk	M	T	W	Th	F	S	S
31							1
32	2	3	4	5	6	7	8
33	9	10	11	12	13	14	15
34	16	17	18	19	20	21	22
35	23	24	25	26	27	28	29
36	30	31					

SEPTEMBER

wk	M	T	W	Th	F	S	S
36			1	2	3	4	5
37	6	7	8	9	10	11	12
38	13	14	15	16	17	18	19
39	20	21	22	23	24	25	26
40	27	28	29	30			

OCTOBER

wk	M	T	W	Th	F	S	S
40					1	2	3
41	4	5	6	7	8	9	10
42	11	12	13	14	15	16	17
43	18	19	20	21	22	23	24
44	25	26	27	28	29	30	31

NOVEMBER

wk	M	T	W	Th	F	S	S
45	1	2	3	4	5	6	7
46	8	9	10	11	12	13	14
47	15	16	17	18	19	20	21
48	22	23	24	25	26	27	28
49	29	30					

DECEMBER

wk	M	T	W	Th	F	S	S
49			1	2	3	4	5
50	6	7	8	9	10	11	12
51	13	14	15	16	17	18	19
52	20	21	22	23	24	25	26
1	27	28	29	30	31		

2022

JANUARY

wk	M	T	W	Th	F	S	S
1						1	2
2	3	4	5	6	7	8	9
3	10	11	12	13	14	15	16
4	17	18	19	20	21	22	23
5	24	25	26	27	28	29	30
6	31						

FEBRUARY

wk	M	T	W	Th	F	S	S
6		1	2	3	4	5	6
7	7	8	9	10	11	12	13
8	14	15	16	17	18	19	20
9	21	22	23	24	25	26	27
10	28						

MARCH

wk	M	T	W	Th	F	S	S
10		1	2	3	4	5	6
11	7	8	9	10	11	12	13
12	14	15	16	17	18	19	20
13	21	22	23	24	25	26	27
14	28	29	30	31			

APRIL

wk	M	T	W	Th	F	S	S
14					1	2	3
15	4	5	6	7	8	9	10
16	11	12	13	14	15	16	17
17	18	19	20	21	22	23	24
18	25	26	27	28	29	30	

MAY

wk	M	T	W	Th	F	S	S
18							1
19	2	3	4	5	6	7	8
20	9	10	11	12	13	14	15
21	16	17	18	19	20	21	22
22	23	24	25	26	27	28	29
23	30	31					

JUNE

wk	M	T	W	Th	F	S	S
23			1	2	3	4	5
24	6	7	8	9	10	11	12
25	13	14	15	16	17	18	19
26	20	21	22	23	24	25	26
27	27	28	29	30			

JULY

wk	M	T	W	Th	F	S	S
27					1	2	3
28	4	5	6	7	8	9	10
29	11	12	13	14	15	16	17
30	18	19	20	21	22	23	24
31	25	26	27	28	29	30	31

AUGUST

wk	M	T	W	Th	F	S	S
32	1	2	3	4	5	6	7
33	8	9	10	11	12	13	14
34	15	16	17	18	19	20	21
35	22	23	24	25	26	27	28
36	29	30	31				

SEPTEMBER

wk	M	T	W	Th	F	S	S
36				1	2	3	4
37	5	6	7	8	9	10	11
38	12	13	14	15	16	17	18
39	19	20	21	22	23	24	25
40	26	27	28	29	30		

OCTOBER

wk	M	T	W	Th	F	S	S
40						1	2
41	3	4	5	6	7	8	9
42	10	11	12	13	14	15	16
43	17	18	19	20	21	22	23
44	24	25	26	27	28	29	30
45	31						

NOVEMBER

wk	M	T	W	Th	F	S	S
45		1	2	3	4	5	6
46	7	8	9	10	11	12	13
47	14	15	16	17	18	19	20
48	21	22	23	24	25	26	27
49	28	29	30				

DECEMBER

wk	M	T	W	Th	F	S	S
49				1	2	3	4
50	5	6	7	8	9	10	11
51	12	13	14	15	16	17	18
52	19	20	21	22	23	24	25
1	26	27	28	29	30	31	

| 28 Monday | Boxing Day, holiday (Christian) |

| 29 Tuesday |

| 30 Wednesday |

| 31 Thursday | New Year's Eve
Hogmanay (Scotland) |

| 1 Friday | New Year's Day
Holiday (UK, Republic of Ireland) |

| 2 Saturday | 3 Sunday |

Settled in *by Ryan Miller*
Moose are not strangers to the city of Anchorage, Alaska. This big bull
is known as Hook, and Ryan knew that he would soon be shedding his
magnificent crown. This scene was captured in heavy snowfall as the rest
of the city slept, and less than an hour later Hook shed his first antler.

January

---

4 Monday

---

5 Tuesday

---

6 Wednesday

---

7 Thursday

---

8 Friday

---

9 Saturday

10 Sunday

The unstoppable force *by Paddy Scott*
Paddy had spent weeks listening to the thunder of snow as it slid from
K6 – initially startled, he gradually became accustomed to the mountain's
roars and transfixed by its endless drama. He was in the Himalayas,
Pakistan, documenting a climbing expedition, when the avalanche struck.

11 Monday

12 Tuesday

13 Wednesday

14 Thursday

15 Friday

16 Saturday

17 Sunday

Land of snow and ice *by Josh Anon*
Josh was on a boat in a fjord across from Longyearbyen, Svalbard,
Norway, when he spotted this polar bear walking along the edge of the
ice. She was curious and walked past the boat twice – just long enough
for Josh to take a shot of her against a glowing Arctic sunset.

January

18 Monday

19 Tuesday

20 Wednesday

21 Thursday

22 Friday

23 Saturday

24 Sunday

Arctic treasure *by Sergey Gorshkov*
Carrying its trophy from a raid on a snow goose nest, an Arctic fox heads
for a suitable burial spot. The soil of Wrangel Island in the Russian Far East,
which is ice-bound for much of the year, stays as cold as a refrigerator so
any cached eggs will remain edible long after they are stored away.

January

25 Monday   Burns Night (Scotland)

26 Tuesday   Australia Day

27 Wednesday

28 Thursday

29 Friday

30 Saturday

31 Sunday

Fire ice *by Chris Bray*
Through the open doors of the helicopter, fighting biting winds and
turbulence, Chris captured the most dramatic sight of all – southern
Iceland's fractured sooty Mýrdalsjökull ice cap, ominously concealing
simmering volcanic fires beneath.

February

1 Monday

2 Tuesday

3 Wednesday

4 Thursday

5 Friday

6 Saturday

7 Sunday

Cold catch *by Fred Zacek*
Emerging onto the ice from its feeding hole in a river in eastern Estonia,
an otter shakes off excess water before eating its catch. Nearby, lying on
the ice, Fred was watching carefully. Each time the otter dived, Fred slid
closer – close enough to hear the otter crunching up the frogs.

8 Monday

9 Tuesday

10 Wednesday

11 Thursday

12 Friday   Chinese New Year (Year of the Ox)

13 Saturday

14 Sunday   Valentine's Day

Arctic blues *by Reiner Leifried*
Set against the backdrop of the snowy landscape, the blue light of the
Arctic winter created a hypnotic atmosphere. Reiner raised his camera
hoping to capture 'calmness with an endless view'. He used the smooth
wave, rippling like folds of satin, from the ship's motion to frame his shot.

February

---

15 Monday   George Washington's Birthday (USA)

---

16 Tuesday   Shrove Tuesday, Pancake Day (Christian)

---

17 Wednesday   Ash Wednesday (Christian)

---

18 Thursday

---

19 Friday

---

20 Saturday	21 Sunday

Realm of the condor *by Klaus Tamm*
Hiking across the challenging terrain of Torres del Paine National Park,
Chile, Klaus had half an eye on the Andean condors soaring above.
Suddenly, one of them dropped down in front of a glacier and Klaus
quickly captured the imposing bird silhouetted against the icy blue peaks.

February

22 Monday

23 Tuesday

24 Wednesday

25 Thursday

26 Friday

27 Saturday

28 Sunday

The look of a whale *by Wade Hughes*
The warm waters off Tonga's Vava'u Islands are the humpback whales'
winter breeding ground. This female had recently given birth and
repeatedly approached Wade, probably sizing him up. Being the subject
of her searching, intelligent gaze was, he says, 'humbling'.

March

1 Monday

2 Tuesday

3 Wednesday

4 Thursday

5 Friday

6 Saturday

7 Sunday

Snow spat *by Erlend Haarberg*
As spring awakens in Norway's upland birch forest, tensions between mountain hares grow. One night, two hares came to blows in front of Erlend's hide, squabbling over food he had left out to attract them. Snowflakes flying, Erlend froze the action.

March

---

8 Monday

---

9 Tuesday

---

10 Wednesday

---

11 Thursday

---

12 Friday

---

13 Saturday

14 Sunday   Mothering Sunday

Sweet-grass and ripples *by Theo Bosboom*
On a blustery day, Theo walked past a lake in Björnlandet National Park,
northern Sweden, on his way to explore the ancient pine forest. Glancing
at the water he noticed 'the beautiful patterns created by the play of the
wind, the waves, the grass and the reflections of the half-clouded sky'.

15 Monday

16 Tuesday

17 Wednesday

St Patrick's Day, holiday (Ireland)

18 Thursday

19 Friday

20 Saturday

Spring Equinox

21 Sunday

Bear hug *by Ashleigh Scully*
Ashleigh fell in love with brown bears on a trip to Alaska's Lake Clark
National Park where she was intent on photographing family life. There
is a strong bond between mother and cub and this one was trying to
wrestle mum to the sand. 'As always, she played along, firm, but patient.'

22 Monday

23 Tuesday

24 Wednesday

25 Thursday

26 Friday

27 Saturday
First day of Passover (Jewish)

28 Sunday
British Summertime begins,
clocks go forward
Palm Sunday (Christian)

Shaking off *by Connor Stefanison*
Every so often, an eruption of snowy owls makes its way down from the
Arctic, where they breed, to the Pacific Northwest of North America,
and gather in areas like Delta, British Columbia. Connor captured this owl
head-on as it was shaking off its feathers on a rainy winter day.

29 Monday

30 Tuesday

31 Wednesday

1 Thursday

April Fools' Day
Maundy Thursday (Christian)

2 Friday

Good Friday, holiday (Christian)

3 Saturday

Last day of Passover (Jewish)

4 Sunday

Easter Sunday (Christian)

Reach for the sky *by Steven Blandin*
Steven was taking pictures of a small group of adult roseate spoonbills in
a rookery in Tampa Bay, Florida, when he noticed a newcomer flying in
from afar. With just enough time to back up a few steps, he photographed
the bird landing with its wings in a stunning symmetrical U-shape.

April

---

5 Monday

---

6 Tuesday

---

7 Wednesday

---

8 Thursday

---

9 Friday

---

10 Saturday | 11 Sunday

Breakfast at dawn *by Jari Heikkinen*
Jari arrived before dawn at the lake near his home in south Finland to
photograph a pair of red-throated divers. The male landed with a skidding
splash right in front of his floating hide, holding breakfast. Light bounced
off ripples, fish and feathers, creating an explosion of sparkles.

12 Monday

---

13 Tuesday

---

14 Wednesday

---

15 Thursday

---

16 Friday

---

17 Saturday

18 Sunday

The jellyfish jockey *by Anthony Berberian*
Anthony regularly dives late at night, far off the island of Tahiti, French
Polynesia, to photograph tiny deep sea creatures that migrate to the
surface in darkness to feed. This lobster larva, protected from stings by its
hard shell, was snacking and riding on a small mauve stinger jellyfish.

19 Monday

20 Tuesday

21 Wednesday   Queen Elizabeth II's birthday

22 Thursday

23 Friday   St George's Day (England)

24 Saturday

25 Sunday   Anzac Day (Australia, New Zealand)

In the grip of the gulls *by Ekaterina Bee*
Ekaterina was on a boat trip off the coast of central Norway, but unlike
her companions, her focus was not on the white-tailed sea eagles, but on
a white cloud of herring gulls attracted by bread. Engrossed, she snapped
this image – a whirlwind of flapping wings, coloured feet and beaks.

April – May

26 Monday

27 Tuesday

28 Wednesday

29 Thursday

30 Friday

1 Saturday

2 Sunday

Hammerhead *by Adriana Basques*
Scalloped hammerhead sharks are generally found in the deep waters off
Cocos Island, Costa Rica. It can be a tough dive, with fierce currents and
poor visibilty, but Adriana had the advantage of a sunny day, clear waters,
and a fortuitous school of cottonmouths as the perfect shark backdrop.

3 Monday

4 Tuesday

5 Wednesday

6 Thursday

7 Friday

8 Saturday

9 Sunday

Kick back and chill *by Alan Chung*
After more than two hours hiking in Volcanoes National Park, Rwanda,
Alan came across a family of 16 mountain gorillas led by a single strong
silverback. They were feeding on young bamboo shoots and relaxing in a
leafy open spot. Their family name is 'Hirwa', meaning 'the lucky one'.

---

10 Monday

---

11 Tuesday

---

12 Wednesday   Ramadan ends (Islamic)

---

13 Thursday   Ascension Day (Christian)

---

14 Friday

---

15 Saturday | 16 Sunday

Glimpse of a lynx *by Laura Albiac Vilas*
Laura travelled to the Sierra de Andújar Nature Park in southern Spain to
follow her dream of seeing wild Iberian lynx. Luckily, on her second day, a
pair were relaxing just metres from the road. 'I felt huge respect to be so
close to them and to observe them so peacefully,' she says.

17 Monday

18 Tuesday

19 Wednesday

20 Thursday

21 Friday

22 Saturday

23 Sunday   Whitsun (Christian)

Warning wings *by Mike Harterink*
Diving in St Eustatius in the Caribbean, Mike used a slow shutter speed
to capture the motion of this 'flying' gurnard. The large pectoral fins are
usually held by the body as it walks the ocean floor but, when threatened,
the fish expands its dappled electric-blue wings to scare away predators.

---

24 Monday

---

25 Tuesday

---

26 Wednesday

---

27 Thursday

---

28 Friday

| 29 Saturday | 30 Sunday | Trinity Sunday (Christian) |

Anticipation *by Marco Urso*
As soon as they saw their mother emerge from the lake carrying a plump sockeye salmon, the cubs rushed towards her. Marco has been coming to Lake Kuril, in Kamchatka, Russia, every summer since 2013 to watch the brown bears and has got to know their different personalities and habits.

---

31 Monday   Spring holiday (UK, Scotland)

---

1 Tuesday

---

2 Wednesday

---

3 Thursday   Corpus Christi (Christian)

---

4 Friday

| 5 Saturday | 6 Sunday |

Rough love *by Edwar Herreno*
When Edwar spotted these guineafowl pufferfish off the northwest coast
of Costa Rica, the large female was cowering in a crevice, surrounded by
a gang of amorous males. Intent on fertilising her eggs, they tugged her
into the open water, where she finally released her eggs.

June

7 Monday

8 Tuesday

9 Wednesday

10 Thursday

11 Friday

12 Saturday

13 Sunday

Grooming the descendant *by Claudio Contreras Koob*
This Caribbean flamingo chick is being preened by one of its parents in
the Ría Lagartos Biosphere Reserve, Mexico. Chicks remain in the nest
for less than a week, then wander around the colony in crèches feeding
themselves, although they depend on their parents for several months.

June

14 Monday

15 Tuesday

16 Wednesday

17 Thursday

18 Friday

19 Saturday

20 Sunday   Father's Day

Father knows best *by Christian Ziegler*
A male southern cassowary shows his six-week-old chicks what to eat
in the tropical forests of Papua New Guinea. He will do all the childcare
for nine months or more (he also incubated the eggs). He is a fearsome
protector – Christian was chased away three times by this territorial male.

June

21 Monday

22 Tuesday

23 Wednesday

24 Thursday

25 Friday

26 Saturday   27 Sunday

The good life *by Daniël Nelson*
Daniël finally caught up with a family of western lowland gorillas in the
forest of Odzala-Kokoua National Park in the Republic of Congo. He hopes
to raise awareness of the species and the forest on which they depend –
here Caco, a feisty nine-year-old, feasts on a fleshy African breadfruit.

28 Monday

29 Tuesday

30 Wednesday

1 Thursday   Canada Day

2 Friday

3 Saturday	4 Sunday	Independence Day (USA)

Limpet exposure *by Theo Bosboom*
It was a long, steep scramble in the dark to catch the blue light before
sunrise on Portugal's Sintra coast. To get both the limpets and jagged
rocks in focus and correctly exposed, Theo merged 21 images. A small
flashlight masked with a handkerchief gave a radiant touch to the limpets.

5 Monday

6 Tuesday

7 Wednesday

8 Thursday

9 Friday

10 Saturday

11 Sunday

Contemplation *by Peter Delaney*
Peter had spent a difficult morning tracking chimpanzees through dense
undergrowth in Uganda's Kibale National Park. When he eventually caught
up with them, Totti was trying to entice a female to join him. His efforts
failed and he flopped onto the floor, worn out with unrequited love.

July

12 Monday

Battle of the Boyne,
holiday (Northern Ireland)

13 Tuesday

14 Wednesday

15 Thursday

St Swithin's Day (Christian)

16 Friday

17 Saturday

18 Sunday

Saguaro twist *by Jack Dykinga*
As the gentle dawn light bathed Arizona's Sonoran Desert, Jack trained
his lens on the distant Sand Tank Mountains. This saguaro cactus had
fallen victim to frost damage, allowing Jack to climb inside. A wide angle
revealed its furrowed arms, perfectly framing its emblematic neighbours.

19 Monday

20 Tuesday

21 Wednesday

22 Thursday

23 Friday

24 Saturday

25 Sunday

Cleaning session *by Jordi Chias Pujol*
The protected waters around Carall Bernat, Medes Islands, Spain, are admired for their marine diversity and are popular with divers. Sunfish visit in the spring to be cleaned by small rainbow wrasses. The sunfish adopt an upright position, signalling to the wrasses that they are ready.

26 Monday

27 Tuesday

28 Wednesday

29 Thursday

30 Friday

31 Saturday	1 Sunday

Sewage surfer *by Justin Hofman*
Justin watched, delighted as this tiny estuary seahorse hopped from
one piece of natural debris to the next on a reef near Sumbawa Island,
Indonesia. But as the tide turned, the mood changed. More and more
unnatural objects appeared and the creature seized upon this cotton bud.

August

2 Monday

3 Tuesday

4 Wednesday

5 Thursday

6 Friday

7 Saturday

8 Sunday

Spring release *by John Mullineux*
John waited by a waterhole in South Africa's Kruger National Park –
drought had heightened tensions and he was hoping to see a crocodile
attack. Wish granted, a crocodile exploded out of the water and, with
lightening speed, all four impalas twisted their bodies away from danger.

9 Monday

10 Tuesday

11 Wednesday

12 Thursday

13 Friday

14 Saturday

15 Sunday

Snap shot *by Rodrigo Friscione Wyssmann*
As Rodrigo dived down into the shallows of Mexico's Chinchorro Bank
Biosphere Reserve, two American crocodiles lunged at one another.
His camera pre-set to shoot into the surface light, and strobes aimed
downwards to minimise backscatter, he captured the fierce energy.

16 Monday

17 Tuesday

18 Wednesday

19 Thursday

20 Friday

21 Saturday

22 Sunday

Freshwater Eden *by Michel Roggo*
Michel was having fun exploring the underwater jungle of a tiny tributary
in the vast Pantanal, Brazil – the world's largest tropical wetland. This
scene, a tangle of water hyacinth, with its diversity of shapes and colours,
reminded him of an impressionist painting.

23 Monday

24 Tuesday

25 Wednesday

26 Thursday

27 Friday

28 Saturday

29 Sunday

Giant gathering *by Tony Wu*
Dozens of sperm whales mingled noisily off Sri Lanka's northeast coast,
stacked as far as Tony could see. Immediately, he realised that this was
something special and hopes that after years of commercial whaling, this
kind of major gathering could be a sign that populations are recovering.

30 Monday   Summer holiday (UK, excluding Scotland)

31 Tuesday

1 Wednesday

2 Thursday

3 Friday

4 Saturday   5 Sunday

Resplendent delivery *by Tyohar Kastiel*
Tyohar watched a pair of quetzals deliver fruit to their chicks in a partly
logged area in the Costa Rican cloud forest of San Gerardo de Dota. The
additional light from the fallen trees made it easier to catch the iridescent
colour of the male's dazzling body plumage and tail streamers.

6 Monday

Labor Day (USA)
Labour Day (Canada)

7 Tuesday

Rosh Hashanah begins, Jewish New Year

8 Wednesday

Rosh Hashanah ends, Jewish New Year

9 Thursday

10 Friday

11 Saturday

12 Sunday

Sloth hanging out *by Luciano Candisani*
Luciano had to climb a cecropia tree, in the protected Atlantic rainforest
of southern Bahia, Brazil, to take an eye-level shot of this three-toed sloth.
Sloths like to feed on the leaves of these trees, and so they are often seen
high up in the canopy.

---

13 Monday

---

14 Tuesday

---

15 Wednesday   Yom Kippur, begins at sundown (Jewish)

---

16 Thursday   Yom Kippur, ends at nightfall (Jewish)

---

17 Friday

---

18 Saturday | 19 Sunday

Circle of life *by Jordi Chias Pujol*
Jordi was diving off the Azores when he got the tip-off – a school of
Atlantic horse mackerel had formed a 5 m (16 ft) baitball and were being
circled by predators. By swimming in a tight, coordinated school, they
confuse their attackers, making it difficult for them to pick out individuals.

September

20 Monday

21 Tuesday

22 Wednesday   Autumn Equinox

23 Thursday

24 Friday

25 Saturday   26 Sunday

Dark side of the plains *by Uri Golman*
Uri had dedicated a whole week to black-and-white photography on the
plains of the Maasai Mara National Reserve in Kenya. After a long day he
came across six giraffes walking in formation, and when three broke off
and headed into the shadows he got this remarkable shot.

September – October

27 Monday

28 Tuesday

29 Wednesday

30 Thursday

1 Friday

2 Saturday

3 Sunday

Dreams in the waves *by Mike Korostelev*
Every autumn walruses swim to this rookery on Cape Vankarem, Chukotka,
Russia. Walking along the beach away from the rookery, Mike came across
this lone walrus sleeping on the shore with its tusks stuck in the sand,
comically propping its head up out of the water.

October

4 Monday

5 Tuesday

6 Wednesday

7 Thursday

8 Friday

9 Saturday

10 Sunday

Black kites, red sunset *by Dhyey Shah*
Dhyey was on a trip to see the vultures in Rajasthan's Jorbeer Conservation
Reserve, India, but he was drawn to a group of black kites roosting in a
tree. He started to experiment with silhouettes and considers this his best
shot, at sunset on an evening when the sky turned a vibrant, dusky red.

October

11 Monday

12 Tuesday

13 Wednesday

14 Thursday

15 Friday

16 Saturday

17 Sunday

Elegant mother and calf *by Ray Chin*
Southern humpback whales migrate north from their Antarctic feeding grounds to give birth in the warm sheltered waters of Tonga. Ray chanced upon this mother and calf peacefully floating. After he gently approached them, they swam a bit closer before they made this elegant turn.

October

18 Monday

19 Tuesday

20 Wednesday

21 Thursday

22 Friday

23 Saturday

24 Sunday

Road hog *by Evalotta Zacek*
Evalotta was out for the evening on one of the family's 'animal drives' in
southern Estonia, looking for deer and foxes to photograph at the edge
of a dusky forest. They stopped the car to allow this wandering hedgehog
to cross the road, and in return it posed for a photo.

25 Monday

26 Tuesday

27 Wednesday

28 Thursday

29 Friday

30 Saturday

31 Sunday

British Summertime ends,
clocks go back
Halloween

Spawn rivals *by David Herasimtschuk*
Every autumn the brook trout start to spawn in rivers across New England.
Unfortunately for David, it meant lying motionless for hours in freezing
water as he watched two suitors attempt to court the female between
them, their warm hues underwater matching those of the leaves above.

November

---

1 Monday

---

2 Tuesday

---

3 Wednesday

---

4 Thursday   Diwali (Sikh, Hindu)

---

5 Friday   Guy Fawkes/Bonfire Night

---

6 Saturday | 7 Sunday

An elegant affair *by Knut Erik Alnæs*
The mesmerising ballet of courting great crested grebes had long
fascinated Knut Erik. Night after night he lay on a muddy bank beside Lake
Østensjøvannet in Oslo, Norway, determined to capture their elegance.
The light was exquisite and on his fifth and final night two birds united.

November

8 Monday

9 Tuesday

10 Wednesday

11 Thursday   Armistice Day

12 Friday

13 Saturday

14 Sunday   Remembrance Sunday

A magnificence of monarchs *by Jaime Rojo*
Jaime had witnessed the spectacular gathering of monarch butterflies
before, but this time he had a permit to stay at the Monarch Butterfly
Biosphere Reserve, Mexico, until dusk. As the sun set, the sacred fir forest
turned gold and the branches drooped with millions of butterflies.

15 Monday

16 Tuesday

17 Wednesday

18 Thursday

19 Friday

20 Saturday

21 Sunday

Wolf watch *by Lasse Kurkela*
After an unsuccessful year looking for Finland's wolves, Lasse heard of a
group attracted by bait for bears and arrived at a remote hide in darkness.
First light revealed movement in the trees. Wrapping his camera in fabric
to silence it, he used black and white to capture the eerie scene.

November

---

22 Monday

---

23 Tuesday

---

24 Wednesday

---

25 Thursday   Thanksgiving (USA)

---

26 Friday

---

27 Saturday

28 Sunday   Hanukkah, Festival of Lights begins (Jewish)

Killer tactics *by George Karbus*
George was freediving in the dark Arctic waters of northern Norway,
watching killer whales stunning fish with their tails before eating them.
Suddenly, the whales regrouped. A minute later, they attacked with a new
strategy, mouths open and flying through the fish at high speed.

29 Monday

30 Tuesday

1 Wednesday

2 Thursday

3 Friday

4 Saturday

5 Sunday

Wings of winter *by Imre Potyó*
Flitting through the bare branches of a dark forest in the Börzsöny Hills
of northern Hungary, a male winter moth seeks romance under the stars.
Imre used a multiexposure technique to freeze its movement and to
capture the starlit forest, multiple bursts of light from a stroboscopic flash.

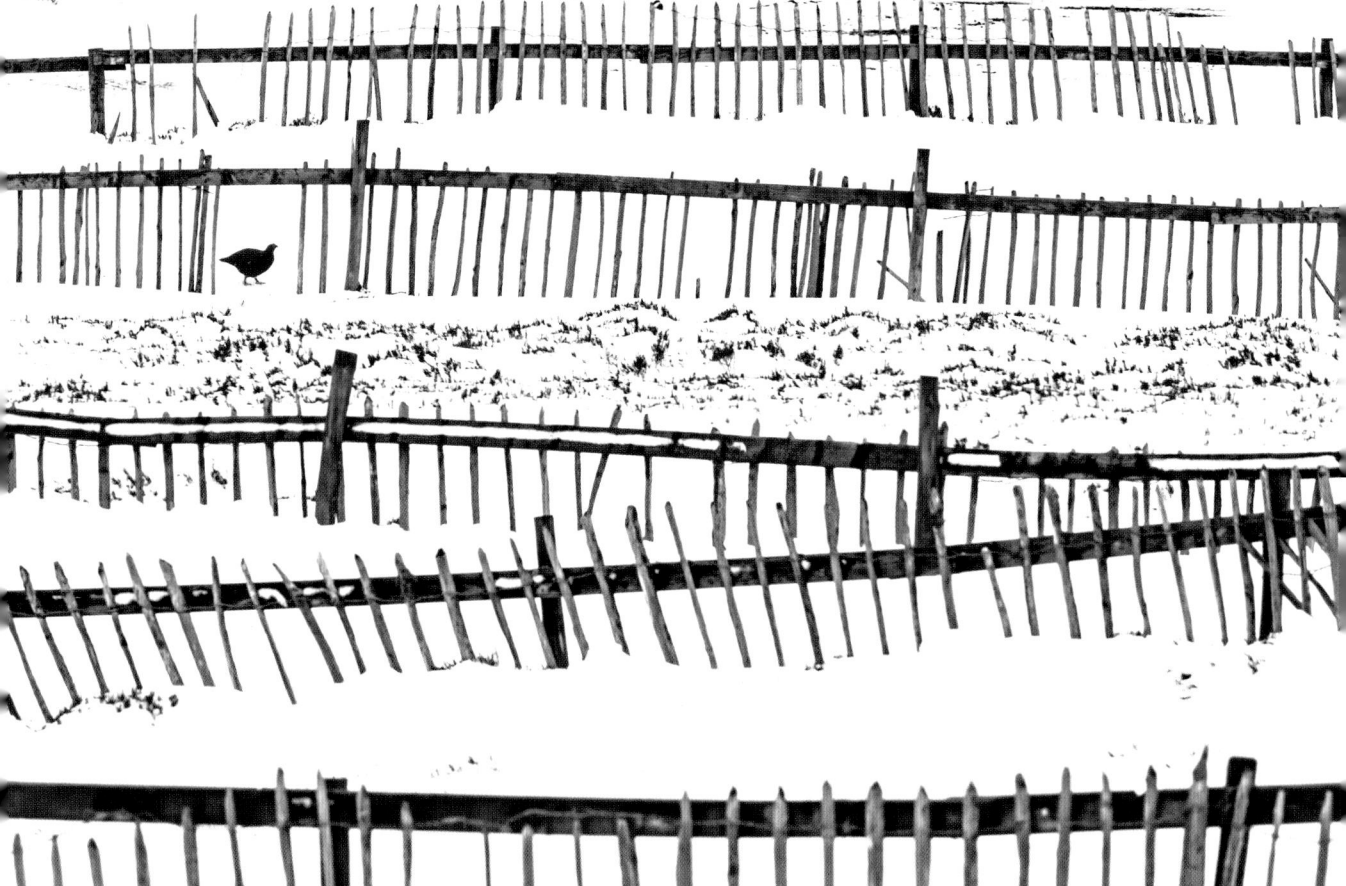

December

---

6 Monday

---

7 Tuesday

---

8 Wednesday

---

9 Thursday

---

10 Friday

---

11 Saturday | 12 Sunday

Off piste *by Hugo Wassermann*
With most of the slopes closed because of lack of snow, the ski resort in
Scotland's Cairngorm National Park attracted a different kind of visitor –
red grouse. This bird ambled at leisure, searching for vegetation, moving
only slightly to make way for the occasional maintenance vehicle.

13 Monday

14 Tuesday

15 Wednesday

16 Thursday

17 Friday

18 Saturday

19 Sunday

Swim gym *by Laurent Ballesta*
Laurent was a few metres from the surface when he heard a strange
noise. Curious, he swam closer to the sound and was met by two Weddell
seals. Using light from the Antarctic ice above, he captured the curious
gaze of the pup, the arc of its body mirroring that of its watchful mother.

December

20 Monday

---

21 Tuesday

Winter Solstice

---

22 Wednesday

---

23 Thursday

---

24 Friday

Christmas Eve (Christian)

---

25 Saturday

Christmas Day (Christian)

26 Sunday

Boxing Day (Christian)

Stuck in *by Ashleigh Scully*
Deep snow had blanketed the Lamar Valley in Yellowstone National Park
and this female red fox was hunting. Every so often she would stop and
listen intently for sound of prey beneath the snow and then leap high in
the air, before punching down, forefeet and nose first and legs upended.

December – January

---

27 Monday   Christmas Day, holiday (Christian)

---

28 Tuesday   Boxing Day, holiday (Christian)

---

29 Wednesday

---

30 Thursday

---

31 Friday   New Year's Eve
                                                 Hogmanay (Scotland)

---

1 Saturday   New Year's Day | **2 Sunday**

Polar pas de deux *by Eilo Elvinger*
From her ship, anchored off Svalbard, in Arctic Norway, Eilo spotted a polar
bear and her two-year-old cub approaching. Mirroring each other, they
stopped to lick a patch of snow soaked in leakage from the vessel's kitchen.
'I was ashamed', says Eilo, 'of how this influenced the bears' behaviour.'

Notes

Notes

Index of photographers

Week 1 (2022)
Polar pas de deux

Eilo Elvinger
Luxembourg
eilo@eilopict.com
Canon EOS-1DX + 200–400mm f4 lens at 200mm; 1/640 sec at f9 (+0.7 e/v); ISO 6400.

Week 33
Snap shot

Rodrigo Friscione Wyssmann
Mexico
rodrigofriscione.com
Nikon D800 + 16–35mm f4 lens at 16mm; 1/250 sec at f6.3; ISO 200; Nauticam housing; two Inon strobes.

Week 39
Dark side of the plains

Uri Golman
Denmark
uri@urigolman.com
Canon EOS-1DX Mark II + Canon 70–200mm f2.8 lens at 180mm; 1/250 sec at f16; ISO 200.

Cover & week 4
Arctic treasure

Sergey Gorshkov
Russia
gorshkov-photo.com
Nikon D300S + 600mm f4 lens; 1/1250 sec at f5; ISO 800; Gitzo tripod + Wimberley head.

Week 10
Snow spat

Erlend Haarberg
Norway
haarbergphoto.com
Nikon D800E + 300mm f2.8 lens; 1/1600 sec at f2.8; ISO 3200; Gitzo tripod + UniqBall head; two 1000W lamps.

Week 21
Warning wings

Mike Harterink
The Netherlands
mike@scubaqua.com
Nikon D200 + 12–24mm f1.4 lens at 12mm; 1/8 sec at f22; ISO 100; Seacam housing; two Seacam flashes.

Week 15
Breakfast at dawn

Jari Heikkinen
Finland
jari.heikkinen@ppq.inet.fi
Nikon D4S + 600mm f4 lens + 1.4x extender; 1/640 sec at f20 (–1.7 e/v); ISO 1600; Manfrotto tripod and video head.

Week 44
Spawn rivals

David Herasimtschuk
USA
freshwatersillustrated.org
Sony A7RII + 28mm f2 lens + Nauticam WWL-1 lens; 1/60 sec at f7.1; ISO 2000; Nauticam housing; two Inon strobes.

Week 23
Rough love

Edwar Herreno
Colombia/Costa Rica
edwarherreno.com
Nikon D300 + Tokina 10–17mm f3.5–4.5 lens at 17mm; 1/125 sec at f8; ISO 200; Sea & Sea housing; two Sea & Sea strobes.

Week 31
Sewage surfer

Justin Hofman
USA
justin-hofman.com
Sony Alpha 7R II + 16–35mm f4 lens; 1/60 sec at f16; ISO 320; Nauticam housing + Zen 230mm Nauticam N120 Superdome; two Sea & Sea strobes with electronic sync.

Week 9
The look of a whale

Wade Hughes
Australia
lookingforwhales.com
Canon 5D + 24–105mm f4 lens; 1/250 sec at f8; ISO 400; Nauticam underwater housing.

Week 48
Killer tactics

George Karbus
Czech Republic/Ireland
georgekarbusphotography.com
Nikon D5 + 16mm f2.8 lens; 1/250 sec at f4.5; ISO 5000; Subal housing.

Week 36
Resplendent delivery

Tyohar Kastiel
Israel
tyohar.org
Canon EOS 5D Mark III + 300mm f2.8 lens; 1/3200 sec at f4; ISO 800.

Week 40
Dreams in the waves

Mike Korostelev
Russia
mkorostelev@gmail.com
Canon EOS 5D Mark II + 24–105mm lens; 1/2000 sec at f6.3; ISO 500.

Week 47
Wolf watch

Lasse Kurkela
Finland
lassekurkela.kuvat.fi
Nikon D4S + 800mm f5.6 VR lens; 1/200 sec at f5.6; ISO 14400; tripod + eki gimbal head.

Week 7
Arctic blues

Reiner Leifried
Germany
reinerleifried-photography.de
Nikon D810 + 14–24mm f2.8 lens at 24mm; 1/500 sec at f8 (–1 e/v); ISO 1000.

Week 1
Settled in

Ryan Miller
USA
explorealaskaphoto.com
Canon EOS 5D Mark III + 100–400mm lens at 135mm; 1/6sec at f5; ISO 2000.

Week 32
Spring release

John Mullineux
South Africa
jmximages@gmail.com
Canon EOS-1D Mark IV + 100–400mm f4.5–5.6 lens; 1/2000 sec at f5.6; ISO 400.

Week 26
The good life

Daniël Nelson
The Netherlands
danielnelson.nl
Canon 6D + Sigma 50–500mm f4.5–6.3 lens at 500mm; 1/30 sec at f6.3; ISO 800.

Week 49
Wings of winter
Imre Potyó
Hungary
poimre@gmail.com
Nikon D90 + Nikkor 50mm f1.8 lens
+ Tamron 10–24mm f3.5–4.5 lens at
11mm; double exposure: 1/15 sec at
f13 + 60 sec at f3.5; ISO 1250; flash;
Manfrotto tripod + UniqBall head.

Week 34
Freshwater Eden
Michel Roggo
Switzerland
roggo.ch
Sony Alpha ILCE-7R + Zeiss FE
16–35mm f4 lens; 1/100 sec at f8; ISO
400; Nauticam housing.

Week 46
A magnificence of monarchs
Jaime Rojo
Spain
rojovisuals.com
Nikon D4 + 70–300mm f4.5–5.6 lens
at 155mm; 1/8 sec at f11; ISO 1250;
Gitzo tripod.

Week 2
The unstoppable force
Paddy Scott
UK
paddyscott.com
Canon EOS 5D Mark III + 70–200mm
f2.8 lens at 173mm; 1/640 sec at f11;
ISO 100.

Week 12
Bear hug
Ashleigh Scully
USA
ashleighscullyphotography.com
Canon 5D Mark III + 500mm f4 lens;
1/1250 sec at f8 (+1 e/v); ISO 1250;
Gitzo tripod.

Week 52
Stuck in
Ashleigh Scully
Canon EOS 7D Mark II + 500mm f4
lens; 1/640 sec at f5.6 (+1.7 e/v); ISO
1000.

Week 41
Black kites, red sunset
Dhyey Shah
India
ketanrinku@yahoo.com
Canon EOS 70D + 100–400mm
f4.5–5.6 lens; 1/500 sec at f5.6; ISO
400.

Week 13
Shaking off
Connor Stefanison
Canada
connorstefanison.com
Canon EOS 1D Mark IV + Canon
500mm f4 lens + 1.4x teleconverter;
1/400 sec at f7.1; ISO 800; Gitzo
tripod.

Week 8
Realm of the condor
Klaus Tamm
Germany
tamm-photography.com
Canon EOS-1DX + 800mm f5.6 lens at
800mm; 1/400 sec at f25 (–1.7 e/v);
ISO 125.

Week 22
Anticipation
Marco Urso
Italy
photoxplorica.com
Canon EOS-1DX + 500mm f4 lens;
1/1250 sec at f6.3; ISO 800; Photoseiki
tripod.

Week 50
Off piste
Hugo Wassermann
Italy
hugo.wassermann@gmail.com
Canon 5D Mark III + 500mm f4 lens;
1.4x extender; 1/160 sec at f29; ISO
1000; Gitzo tripod.

Week 35
Giant gathering
Tony Wu
USA
tony-wu.com
Canon EOS 5D Mark III + 15mm f2.8
lens; 1/250 sec at f6.3; ISO 800; Zillion
housing + Pro-One optical dome port.

Week 43
Road hog
Evalotta Zacek
Estonia
zacekfoto.ee
Nikon D7100 + Nikkor 70–200mm
f2.8 lens at 200mm; 1/40 sec at f2.8;
ISO 1600.

Week 6
Cold catch
Fred Zacek
Estonia
zacekfoto.ee
Nikon D810 + Nikkor 300mm f2.8 lens;
1/1000 sec at f2.8; ISO 1600; Gitzo
tripod.

Week 25
Father knows best
Christian Ziegler
Germany
zieglerphoto@gmail.com
Canon EOS 5D Mark II + 16–40mm
f2.8 lens at 16mm; 1/40 sec at f8;
ISO 640; three Canon flashes; remote
release.

First published by the Natural History Museum, Cromwell Road, London SW7 5BD.
© The Trustees of the Natural History Museum, London 2020. All Rights Reserved.
Photographs © the individual photographers.
Text based on original captions used in the Wildlife Photographer of the Year exhibitions.
ISBN: 978 0 565 09490 4

All rights reserved. No part of this publication may be transmitted in any form or by any
means without prior permission of the publisher.
A catalogue record for this book is available from the British Library.
Printed by Toppan Leefung Printing Ltd. China.

Every effort has been made to ensure the accuracy of listed holiday dates, however,
some may have changed after publication for official or cultural reasons.